MISSION: SISTERHOOD!

Girl Scouts of the USA

Chair, National Board of Directors	Chief Executive Officer	Chief Operating Officer	Vice President, Program
Connie L. Lindsey	**Anna Maria Chávez**	**Jan Verhage**	**Eileen Doyle**

PHOTOGRAPHS
Page 54: Kevin Focht
Page 62: Megan McNamara

The women mentioned in this book are examples of how women have used their voice in the world. This doesn't mean that GSUSA (or you) will agree with everything they have ever done or said.

This publication was made possible by a generous grant from the Dove Self-Esteem Fund.

SENIOR DIRECTOR, PROGRAM RESOURCES: Suzanne Harper

ART DIRECTOR: Douglas Bantz

WRITERS: Andrea Vander Pluym, Andrea Bastiani Archibald, Laura J. Tuchman, Valerie Takahama

EXECUTIVE EDITOR: Laura J. Tuchman

ILLUSTRATOR: Susy Pilgrim Waters

DESIGNERS: Pamela Geismar and Kathleen Dames for Charette Communication Design

CONTRIBUTOR: Tommi Lewis Tilden

ART AND PRODUCTION: Ellen Kelliher, Sarah Micklem, Sheryl O'Connell, Lesley Williams

© 2010 by Girl Scouts of the USA

First published in 2010 by Girl Scouts of the USA
420 Fifth Avenue, New York, NY 10018-2798
www.girlscouts.org

ISBN: 978-0-88441-753-8

Printed in Italy

6 7 8 9/18 17 16 15

Text printed on Fedrigoni Cento 40 percent de-inked, post-consumer fibers and 60 percent secondary recycled fibers. Covers printed on Prisma artboard FSC Certified mixed sources.

FSC
www.fsc.org
MIX
Paper from responsible sources
FSC® C115118

Mission: Sisterhood!

5 Welcome to *Mission: Sisterhood!*

10 Me + Friendship

24 Be My Own Best Friend

36 Buddy Up for Sisterhood

46 Friendship Without Borders

58 Circle the World for Sisterhood

Welcome to
MISSION: SISTERHOOD!

SISTERHOOD. IT'S FOUND IN THOSE SPECIAL moments of real connection you experience with girlfriends, your mother, sisters, aunts, and female cousins (and, yes, your Girl Scout sisters!)—and all the connections you *will* experience with all the girls and women you have yet to meet!

Sisterhood isn't just hanging out with good female friends. It's not just sharing a joke or confiding in someone you trust. Sisterhood is so much deeper than that. It's an authentic connection you feel when you and other females relate to one another on a level you all recognize in your gut as being different and apart from even those connections you share with others dear to you. These sisterhood moments may spring from something serious, such as a shared concern, or they may be triggered by something silly. Either way, the moment, and the connection it carries, is significant and heartfelt.

That's why sisterhood can offer so much to your life, and your story. A sisterhood moment has the power to make you feel good—about yourself and your place in the world. Collectively, sisterhood moments expand your potential and give you the power to see your own life story. And as you grow your story, you can better shape the story for all women and girls. Sisterhood is an expanding spiral that starts with you and then circles out!

So what are your sisterhood stories? On this journey, you'll uncover them. You'll create new sisterhood stories, too. You'll decide what a sisterhood issue is and explore some around you. Whatever you do, big or small, now or throughout your life, it will be all the stronger with the power of sisterhood behind it.

Sisterhood is *multigenerational, multiracial— multi*-anything!

Sist•ry

There are many ways that women and girls join together and bond through sisterhood: college sororities; prayer groups; the women's rights movement; quilting circles; and Girl Scouts.

Girl Scouting was founded on the friendship of girls and women, and their shared experiences and concerns. After all, all women and girls are connected, right? Just thinking about that gives new power and meaning to the Connect key of the Girl Scout Leadership Experience! And connecting through a sisterhood doesn't require high-speed Internet— but it can sometimes help!

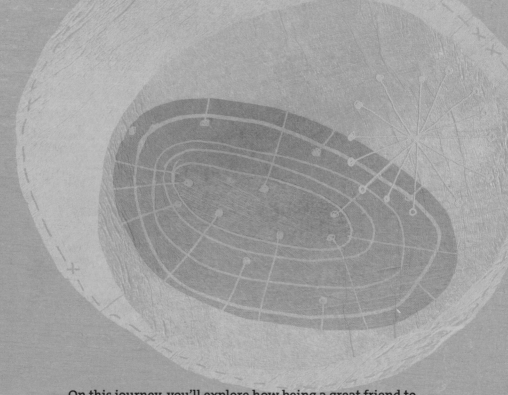

On this journey, you'll explore how being a great friend to yourself is really the best way to start your circle of sisterhood. Then you'll expand your circle! As you do, you'll feel your confidence soar and you'll make new connections. These friendships will enrich your life—and the lives of others—in ways you've never imagined!

Your mission:
Sisterhood!

Your motto:
What starts with Me Can Change the World!

Your Bonus Mission,
Should You Choose to Accept It:
Earn the
Sisterhood Award!

Sisterhood has the power to lift up everything you do! Imagine harnessing all that power to make a difference in the world. You can earn a Girl Scout leadership award by doing that—through a Sisterhood Project. But even more rewarding is how you'll feel when you **reach Mission: Accomplished!** You will have created real change for sisterhood. How?

By defining a sisterhood issue for yourself, creating a plan for how to Take Action on that issue, and then Taking Action!

You decide what speaks to you!

You will find something you want to change for the better for girls around you or around the world—maybe something you haven't really had a chance to think about before.

Want to start a bully-prevention program for younger Girl Scouts? Ask your Girl Scout volunteer or council about the BFF (Be a Friend First) experience for Cadettes. Perhaps you could help younger girls learn how to deal with this serious issue.

Want to help build schools for girls in other countries? Maybe you're not sure what you want to do. Don't worry! This journey is all about figuring out what you might want to do!

Whatever cause you choose, you'll tap into your existing network of friends and community experts, expand that network, widen your sisterhood circle, and enrich your life!

Ready to create some change?

Flip to the Sisterhood Project Planner on pages 68–77. It gives you all the steps to the Sisterhood Award, great tips, and plenty of space to keep track of all you do along the way.

Throughout this journey, the Sisterhood Award icon (at right) will point you to examples of Sisterhood Projects that may interest you or serve as inspiration for your own Sisterhood Project. So read them all, but choose your own.

Remember:

It's your issue, your sisterhood, your story, your award! Your mission starts now!

GOING FOR GOLD?

Earning the Sisterhood Award will give you the planning skills and experience you need to carry out a Girl Scout Gold Award project that moves you to the top of the Girl Scout leadership ladder! Now, that's something to be proud of, sister!

ME+

FRIENDSHIP

chapter 1

FRIENDS. THEY'RE YOUR BEST CHEERLEADERS, your backstop, your go-to for advice. They're also someone to hang out with, bounce ideas off of, voice your true opinions to. Face it, friends are the many characters that play out in your life story.

So what else do friends do for you? And what can different kinds of friends—from all walks of life—do for you? Well, the more kinds of friends you have, and the more diverse those friends are, the richer your world can be! Friends open you to new points of view, new experiences, new interests, and new opportunities—and even more new friends!

But before you can broaden your friendship circle, it's best to consider who you really are as a friend right now. Say you had to write your friendship story today. How would you start the first chapter?

Ask yourself: *What kind of friend am I? What qualities do I offer as a friend? Do I open myself to new friendships? Do I allow my friends to speak their mind? Do I talk about any of my friends behind their back? What qualities do I look for in my friends, and what does this say about me? Do I favor friends who always agree with me? Who dress well? Who know the popular kids?*

The Many Faces of Friendship

Consider the many types of friends listed on this page. You can be all or some of these to various people at various times, or even at the same time, just as the design indicates. So how many of these friendship types are you? Which are already in your friendship circle? Which would you like to add?

A friend can also be tied to various purposes, such as those listed on the opposite page. The connections between friendship types and purposes can vary. How many can you find in your own life?

Acquaintance: Someone you're friendly with and know by name, but don't know too much about (many friendships begin as acquaintances)

Good friend: Someone with whom you share interests and enjoy spending time, even one on one, but your connection goes only so far—she's just not the one you share your truest feelings with

Group friend: Someone you hang out with and have a good time with as part of a larger group of friends, or a sport or other interest group—but your conversations don't necessarily go too deep

Confidante: Someone you tell your deepest secrets and wildest dreams, and trust she will not divulge them (you turn to her in times of trouble and you know she always has your back)

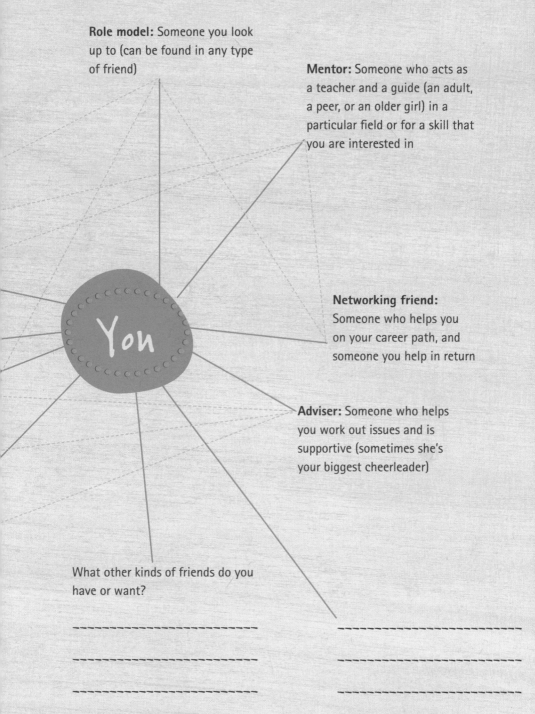

Role model: Someone you look up to (can be found in any type of friend)

Mentor: Someone who acts as a teacher and a guide (an adult, a peer, or an older girl) in a particular field or for a skill that you are interested in

Networking friend: Someone who helps you on your career path, and someone you help in return

You

Adviser: Someone who helps you work out issues and is supportive (sometimes she's your biggest cheerleader)

What other kinds of friends do you have or want?

------------------------------   ------------------------------

------------------------------   ------------------------------

------------------------------   ------------------------------

Friendship potpourri

The yellow rose is known as a friendship rose because yellow is associated with the positive feelings of warmth, joy, and friendship. Just as a diversity of friends makes life more beautiful and interesting, a variety of elements make for the most fragrant potpourri! So start with yellow rose petals as your base and experiment! Here's an easy way to begin a friendship potpourri: Collect about four cups of yellow rose petals, spread them on top of newspaper and allow to dry for two to three days. Then, place the dried rose petals in a jar with a lid. Add several drops of rose oil, seal the jar, and store it in a cool, dry place for at least two weeks, making sure to gently toss the mixture around in the jar every other day. For spice, add nutmeg, bay leaves, cloves, and pinecones to the mix. At the end of two weeks, pour the potpourri into a bowl or other container and present it to a friend!

Finesse Your Friendship **Style**

Just as there are many types of friendships, there are also many friendships styles. With some friends, you may be the life of the party. With others, you may prefer keeping your thoughts to yourself. Depending who you're with, you may lean one way or another.

Have you ever considered how your friendship style can be most effective when meeting new people? If you tend to be energetic, be mindful that you might need to tone yourself down at times to gain the trust and understanding of someone new. If you're more reserved, here are some easy ways to broaden your friendship borders:

- Approach new people in small, quiet settings. (If you're in a large gathering, move the conversation to a quieter space.)

- Meet people through activities, like soccer, theater, or a book club. Shared interests go a long way toward building friendships.

- Ask a lot of questions!

- Smile! A smile will put people at ease and show that you're open to new connections.

- Double-check your body language so that it says you are welcoming—unfold your arms, nod your head, and relax your shoulders.

Science of Sisterhood

Studies of college students show that people who *act* energetic and assertive report that they feel happier and more positive, and have more fun! Give it a try:

- Sing along, out loud, to a song on the radio.
- Ask a question in class.
- Be the first to volunteer for an activity.
- Strike up a conversation with someone you barely know.

Measure of
Friendship

How healthy are your friendships? You may think they're just fine. But on closer look, are your friends boosting you up or bringing you down? Take a look at the chart on the next page and its descriptions of what your closest friends may or may not do. Go through each column and check each item that truly describes your friends.

Noticing a lot of checks in the right-hand column? You're on your way to healthy friendships! You have friends who make you feel safe and supported but aren't afraid to give you constructive feedback when needed. With these friends, you feel you can voice your opinion, try new things, and be the real you! Keep up the good work. You attract friends who make friendship worthwhile.

Noticing a bunch of checks in the left-hand column? You've got some friendship work to do! You have friends who aren't letting you be you! Wouldn't you like to have friends who respect you, encourage you, and give you honest feedback in a positive way when you need it? With friends like these, you *could* voice your opinion, try new things, and be the real you! So start, in small ways, to tell your current friends what you want and need in a friendship. And try expanding your friendship borders to include some new people who fit the descriptions in the right-hand column. The tips on page 15 will get you started.

When women bond together in a community in such a way that "sisterhood" is created, it gives them an accepting and intimate forum to tell their stories and have them heard and validated by others. The community . . . encourages them to grow into their larger destiny.
—Sue Monk Kidd, author, *The Secret Life of Bees*

Your friend ...

- ○ Is critical about your looks or clothing
- ○ Makes fun of you, then says "I'm only kidding!"
- ○ Pretends to hit you, or punches/slaps your arm in a playful but hard way
- ○ Talks over you, or doesn't allow you to speak
- ○ Isn't interested in your goals or interests
- ○ Encourages you to do things that you don't want to do, or that might be harmful or unhealthy
- ○ Wants you to join in when she's disrespecting or bullying others, or spreading rumors
- ○ Is not one to be trusted with anything important to you
- ○ Is mostly concerned with commenting on what's wrong with other people
- ○ Gets angry or threatened when you hang out with others
- ○ Makes you feel stupid for having a belief that's different from her own
- ○ Holds you back from trying new things
- ○ -------------------------
- ○ -------------------------

Your friend ...

- ○ Comments on your looks or clothing only when you ask for honest feedback, or to offer an occasional compliment
- ○ Gives you constructive feedback in positive ways
- ○ Shows she respects you by never touching your body in a mock-violent way
- ○ Is always interested in what you have to say
- ○ Is supportive of your goals and interests
- ○ Is respectful of your health, needs, and boundaries
- ○ Reaches out to others who are made fun of or who are the subject of rumors
- ○ Can be counted on to have your back at all times
- ○ Likes to talk about a multitude of things, from books to sports to news
- ○ Thinks it's cool that you have different friends
- ○ Is interested in your beliefs and ways of thinking
- ○ Helps you grow and encourages you to seek new challenges
- ○ -------------------------
- ○ -------------------------

A Long-Running, and Healthy, Friendship

Sharmin, left, and Shanaz Mahmud

Sharmin and **Shahnaz**. Shahnaz and Sharmin. That's the way it has always been with the Mahmud sisters. Even when they were little, their bond was so strong that people mistook them for twins, despite their three-year age difference. "My mom loves to tell stories about how I always had to have the same clothes as my sister, so people thought we were twins," says Shahnaz, the younger sister. The sisters, whose parents emigrated from Bangladesh, were raised in Durham, Connecticut, in the 1970s. Back then, Durham had few Bangladeshi immigrants. "We leaned on each other for support," Sharmin recalls.

After college, when Sharmin got a job in New York City, it seemed natural for her to move in with Shahnaz, who had an apartment in the city. As the sisters established their careers, they explored the city's cultural offerings together. Shahnaz introduced Sharmin to classic movies projected outdoors at Bryant Park in the summertime. Sharmin took Shahnaz to see the New York City Ballet at Lincoln Center.

"I think we were

lucky," Shahnaz says. "People sometimes say that your friends can be closer than your family because you get to choose your friends. I think if we weren't family, we would have found each other some other way."

Then, after nine years together, Shahnaz, a journalist, moved to London for her work. During a visit, Sharmin was amazed at her sister's transformation. "In our family, she's the baby, the younger sister. But seeing her blossom as a woman and being independent, I was in awe of her," says Sharmin, the director of special events for the Abyssinian Development Corporation in Harlem.

Since Sharmin married in 2007 and moved to the New York borough of Queens, the sisters, once again both living in New York, have found a new way to maintain their bond—and stay in shape. Shahnaz helps her older sister train to run the New York City Marathon. They get together nearly every Sunday morning for a run in Central Park, often followed by brunch at a diner.

They plan to compete in the marathon in 2011 (Sharmin ran it it 2009), and have run warm-up races to prepare. "In a few races, when I haven't been able to keep up, I've told her, 'Just go!,'" Sharmin says. "I want her to be able to race. I want her to run and see how fast she can go." Now, that's being a true sister!

The Science of Sisterhood

Exercise is one of the best ways to clear your mind and keep your whole body healthy. It increases levels of serotonin, the hormone that regulates your mood and increases your sense of well-being. Studies even show that strenuous exercise seems easier and more enjoyable when done with friends. So try this sisterly idea for some friendly exercise:

Farklek: This funny name, based on the Swedish word for "speed play," is a type of interval training in which the pace varies from run to jog to walk. You and a friend can chat while you walk, then compete in a sprint, slow to a jog, and return to a talk-and-walk mode.

Finding the Beauty in Images *of* Beauty

You probably know that the images of perfect-looking girls and women in magazines and on billboards are not reality. In fact, most of those photographs have been retouched to create that perfect-looking image. And most fashion models are thinner than 98 percent of American women!

You probably also know that the portrayals of friendships among girls and women in movies and TV sometimes are not very real either. Too often women and girls are shown to be fickle, catty, backbiting, and just plain mean. Don't you wish these portrayals had been retouched to show the power and beauty of true friendship?

If This Issue Speaks to You, Get Others Involved!

First, think about the beauty ideals (and lack of friendship ideals) that you and other girls are seeing played out in movies and on TV. Talk about these images of girls and friendships with your sister Seniors. Then, with friends, find two films or TV shows (one from the United States and one from another country) that include girls who are friends, and see if and how the characters portray beauty in themselves and in their relationships, especially with other girls and women. You can find films and shows on cable channels, DVDs, and online.

As you watch, you and your friends might ask yourselves:

What beauty ideals are shared among the girls and women?

Of the so-called images of beauty being shown, are the majority about outer beauty or inner beauty?

In what ways are beauty ideals portrayed in films and shows from other countries different from those you see in U.S. films? In what ways are they the same?

Now consider the friendships portrayed among the girls and women.

How do the characters treat one another?

Which of their behaviors are truly friendship ideals? How would you change their behavior with friends so that it would exemplify the positive and strong nature of true friendship?

What differences do you see in friendship stories from other countries?

Did you find some films or TV shows that portrayed girls realistically? If you did, consider writing to the producers to tell them how the film or show matched your reality and why that is so important to you. Encourage them to make more like it! All your sisters who viewed the film or show with you should sign the letter, too. Remember, there's power in numbers! So educate others by sharing the positive and accurate depictions from the film or show. They might sign the letter, too!

If you didn't find accurate portrayals in the film or show you watched, you know what to do! Share your concerns with the producers and get others to join in with you!

Expand This into a Sisterhood Project

You might think of several ways to do this! For example, you might start an ongoing Friday night film club at your school that gives girls an opportunity to view films (prescreened by you) that offer powerful and positive images of girls and women and their relationships.

☐ Get a list of movies going and decide how and where you will show them.

☐ Decide who your audience will be (all girls at school? a specific grade level? teachers? Don't forget the guys—after all, it's important for guys to see real images of women and girls; and girls can't change their reality without the support of the other half of the world!).

☐ Make a plan to get the word out (fliers? posters? e-mail blast? announcement over the PA system?).

☐ Decide on refreshments (movie fare? popcorn and ...?).

Keep Your Sisterhood Going!

Don't let the spirit of your movie night end! If you want to create lasting change, think about all the ways you might do that. For example, you could become a "citizen journalist" and regularly check TV and film Web sites to add comments whenever a comment box is provided. Or you could find out where to e-mail comments, send yours, and get others to send comments, too. If you find a show that is exemplary, let your voice be heard by creating your version of a Humanitas Prize, an annual award given to film and television writers whose work explores the human condition in meaningful ways that educate and inspire. Get your friends together and brainstorm other creative ways to keep positive and powerful images of women and girls growing.

BE MY OWN

BEST FRIEND

chapter 2

BEING HEALTHY, IN MIND AND BODY,

means being a great friend to yourself. When you're your own best friend, you put your best self forward in all areas of life. With your best self forward, you enjoy even stronger friendships, and you have the ability to make new friends with ease.

Friends do a lot of talking. So you probably talk to your best friend (you!) all the time. What kind of messages are you sending yourself?

For one week, every day, pay close attention to the script playing in your head. We're talking detective-level attention here. On Day 1, for a half hour in the morning, pay attention to everything you're telling yourself. What thoughts go through your mind as you're brushing your teeth, looking in the mirror, showering, choosing an outfit, getting dressed, checking the weather, eating breakfast, running on the soccer field? **What stories are you actually telling yourself?**

On Day 2, step up your close listening to a full hour—also pay attention to your inner conversations during math class, at lunch, when you go to the bathroom, when you talk to friends. What kind of voice are you hearing in these various situations? Are you being kind and supportive or are you talking down to yourself? Do you criticize other girls' looks or smarts, or do you look for the good in them?

Consider keeping up the detective work for an hour a day for a whole week. At the end of the week, take stock of all your inner conversations. Did you hear positive thoughts? Negative ones? Something in between? If you heard negativity, don't beat yourself up for it! Just acknowledge it, let it go, and then focus on something more positive. For example, say you saw your reflection in a storefront window and thought, "My thighs look so huge in these shorts! What was I thinking wearing them?" That's not something you would say to a good friend, right? No way!

So talk to yourself like a good friend, too. Say something like, "That thought might have some truth to it, but I don't need to say it out loud. I'm going to focus on the positive. The next window I pass, I'm going to look for my reflection and notice all that's positive about myself today—the way my eyes smile, the cool belt I used to pull my outfit together, the energy in my step!" Remember that even small shifts in the way you talk to yourself can change your view of yourself and your outlook on life in big ways.

Body Buddy

An important part of being your own best friend is choosing to be with friends who support a healthy attitude. Good friends are those who inspire and encourage you to:

- nourish your body with a variety of healthful foods, fresh air and exercise, and rest

- steer clear of toxins—inside and outside your body

- respect what your mind and body are telling you about what's right and not right for you

- appreciate you for you, including all your unique features, your shape, size, and strengths

Friends Matter!

Seventy percent of females say that having a close circle of friends is important to making a woman feel beautiful. In another separate study, the same percentage of girls said that friends are the biggest influence on how they feel about their bodies.

British Medical Journal, *The Dove White Paper Study: Beyond Stereotypes*, 2005

Knowing Your
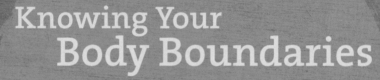
Body Boundaries

As you strengthen your friendship with yourself, be mindful of your personal boundaries. These are your limits for what is OK and what is not OK for you. Say, for example, you don't like people to come up from behind and surprise you by putting their hands over your eyes. Or perhaps you don't like people to come up and talk right in your face.

When things like this happen, does a little alarm go off in your head? That's perfectly fine! You're allowed to have boundaries. They're what keep you comfortable and confident. So be sure to listen to your boundaries.

The more you pay attention to your boundaries, the better you can express them to others, and the more confident and comfortable you'll be.

Wake-Up Call

You and your sister Seniors are busy and constantly on the go. Here are some fun and fast recipes, and space to write your own, for that most important meal on the run—breakfast! Make an extra one or two, wrap them securely (reusable containers are best!), and pass them along to a few breakfast-dodging friends! Just be sure to check for allergies first!

A.M. Pizza

Fresh, sliced tomatoes, low-fat mozzarella, and a handful of spinach on a whole-wheat English muffin. Broil till the cheese melts, then enjoy.

Power Sandwich

Nut butter (aim for almond because it's one of the most healthful nuts) and sliced bananas on whole-grain toast. Top with a sprinkling of granola!

Add your own!

_____

_____

_____

_____

Defining *You*

To be authentic and to honor the things you believe in, you need to be clear about where *you* stand. Your opinion, values, likes, and dislikes may change over time, and that's fine. What's important is to stay true to yourself. But sometimes we adopt our friends' values and follow their interests, rather than staying true to our own.

Think about your usual activities and hobbies, how you act and treat people, the music you listen to, the clothes you wear, and so on. How many of these choices are ones that you've made on your own, and how many reflect your friends' choices?

The Science of Sisterhood

Researchers find that when women get together and bond (like chatting together), a stress-reducing chemical called oxytocin is released in their brains. So chat it up to relax! (But remember: no gossip!)

	Totally Me	Maybe More My Friends' Influence
Clothes	◯	◯
Music	◯	◯
Food	◯	◯
Friends to Hang Out with at Lunchtime	◯	◯
Places to Go on the Weekend	◯	◯
Favorite After-School Activities	◯	◯
	◯	◯
	◯	◯
	◯	◯
	◯	◯

Call *Out* That
Inner Beauty!

Ever notice how often girls greet girls with "I like that sweater," "Love that necklace," or "Your hair looks great"? It's easy to comment on something you see—and it's a quick opportunity to say something nice. But when girls comment only on outer appearance, it sends the message that a girl's looks are more important than her inner attributes. You can turn this inside-out so that your conversations move to more meaningful observations, like how you admire your friend's confidence in class, or how you respect that she refuses to spread rumors.

The more you and your friends focus on aspects that go beyond outer appearance—such as kindness and generosity, or valuable skills such as athletic ability or math prowess—the more you'll appreciate your strengths and differences.

Try It for Fun

For one week, without telling anyone, keep track of three things:

- How many times you and your friends comment on one another's outer appearance. What types of comments are being made?
- How many times you and your friends comment on one another's inner qualities. What types of comments are being made?
- How many times you comment on one another's outer appearance or inner qualities with your male friends. What types of comments are being made, and how do they differ from the ones you exchange with your girlfriends?

If This Issue Speaks to You, Get Others Involved!

Now get your friends together and tell them—without getting into specifics of who said what—how often appearance was mentioned in conversation. Get a discussion going about how focusing daily conversations on exterior beauty can harm a girl's self-worth and hinder her from becoming as confident and capable as she can be.

Determine the status of this issue in your community by asking your friends to join with you in ...

- comparing the difference (if there is one) between how often your girl friends and your guy friends mention appearance in daily conversations.

- discussing what you and your friends consider ideal beauty and where that ideal comes from (fashion magazines? TV shows? movies? music videos?).

- suggesting ways your friends can move their conversation from outer beauty to inner beauty. Ask them to consider whether a friend is beautiful when ...

    she stands up for her beliefs or gut instinct. If so, tell her you admire her strength and courage!

    she carries herself with an inner confidence. If so, tell her how much you admire her self-assured manner.

    she avoids speaking negatively about other girls. If so, let her know how her integrity supports sisterhood and prevents rumors.

    she has other traits, skills, or talents you admire. Is she kind, sporty, funny, gutsy, great in math? Tell her!

If a situation really calls for commenting on a friend's outward appearance, tie it to her personality. Example: "Pairing the plaid and stripes in your outfit is so cool. Your style is always so unique."

After the discussion, start a contest among your friends to see who can curb outward appearance comments the most. Keep track of the number of outer-appearance and inner-appearance comments you hear and compare them to your count from before the group discussion. Were you able to make a measurable difference? Was it easy or tough to do? Why?

Expand This into a Sisterhood Project!

Start an inner beauty campaign to spread the word about the positive power of turning conversations and comments about beauty "inside out."

- **First, choose your audience.** Will it be peers, younger girls, all women and girls? What's best for your community?

- **Next, decide how to best educate and inspire your audience!** For example, with your chosen audience in mind, you might put together a fact sheet about why inner beauty matters and how girls (and/or women) can change their focus from outer beauty to inner beauty.

- **Decide how and to whom you will distribute your fact sheet.** All the girls in your school? At neighboring schools, too? A group of younger girls?

Body Talk

Your body image is the degree to which you feel your body is attractive. Have you ever had a friend who insists she's fat, even though her weight is perfectly healthy for her height? Or a friend who is totally attractive but thinks she needs a nose job? Or maybe you've felt like this? When the conversation (even the one inside your head!) turns to commenting on outer appearance, remind yourself and others that one's looks say little to nothing about who a person really is.

Keep Your Sisterhood Going!

Want to step things up a notch? Consider hosting a communitywide "inner beauty makeover," where girls learn and practice inside-out commentary with fun role-play activities and games.

You might even invite girls to dress in outlandish costumes and see if they can still maintain their focus on inner beauty.

Want to grow it even wider and keep it going longer? Create an online site so you can continue to educate and inspire girls and spread the word to even more girls beyond your region.

BUDDY UP FOR SISTERHOOD

chapter 3

YOU'VE SEEN HOW BEING YOUR OWN BEST
friend can make you happy and confident, and keep you healthy,
too! But think about how great it is to have someone else to turn to,
someone you can count on, someone to laugh with and share life's
ups and downs, someone you can be your true self with. That's why
your friendships—especially those you experience with just one other
person—are so important.

Of course, a lot of friendship is trial and error. It's like testing the
ocean temperature with your toes. If it's not too cold, you're willing
to walk in a bit deeper. Explore your various friendships, new and old,
in a similar way: Start with one question or conversation, then give
something back, even if it's just a listening ear, or a compliment. With
so many levels and types of friendships available to you, you may want
to explore them all! Which ones offer the possibility of expanding your
sisterhood? Which ones add richness to your sisterhood and therefore
to your life?

Take Your Friendship
Up a Notch

If you think a friendship has the potential to move up a level, here are some tips for moving it forward and strengthening it:

Use Your Voice

Don't assume that your friend totally gets you. If you think she doesn't, talk to her! Friends are not mind readers. When you need to discuss a sensitive subject, talk to her in person or by phone. Avoid relying on e-mail, texts, IM, or social networking sites because your tone could be misinterpreted. If you must write your message, wait a day—or longer—before sending it. That way you'll have a chance to double-check that what you've written is what you really intend to say.

Spread Respect

Got a friend who likes to trash talk about other friends with you? Let her know that's just not OK with you, and that if she has a problem with a friend she should talk directly with that friend. You'll also be sending a message that disrespecting girls is not OK.

2 Friends spur a Movement

Girl Scouts started with a friendship forged between an American, Juliette "Daisy" Gordon Low, and a Brit, Robert Baden-Powell.

Baden-Powell led Boy Scouting adventures in India and Africa before formally creating Boy Scouts in England. Daisy met him in London and was intrigued by his experience—he had created the guidelines, rules, and activities for Boy Scouts. Daisy decided to start a Girl Guide troop in Scotland and later, when Baden-Powell traveled to America, Daisy joined him with the intent of starting Girl Guides there, too. Now, a century later, Girl Scouting is all about leadership for girls—leadership in daily life and leadership for the future.

Hear with *Heart*

Being a good friend means being a good listener, so when your friend is sharing something important:

- Show her you're receptive and paying attention (by maintaining good eye contact, leaning forward with your arms and legs uncrossed—and turning off your cell phone)

- Acknowledge that you hear and understand her loud and clear

Active listening will strengthen your relationship because it creates trust. You don't have to agree with what the person has to say, but you'll have heard it.

Birds of a Feather Flock Together

Proverbs the world over express the idea that people who are similar tend to hang out together. Yet open any history book and you'll find that some of the most effective leaders reached out beyond their inner circle. They listened to the stories of all people, and got to know those people on one or a number of friendship levels.

Two Friends,
a Guide for Many

Ada Miller Robinson and Bonnie Jackson Mitchell believe that healthy communication and the power of listening play a key role in healthy friendships. The two met around 1973, when both worked for a Girl Scout Council in Jackson, Mississippi.

"At that time," Ada recalls, "black girls and white girls were in segregated troops. But our council didn't care and mixed the girls up. We were still on the heels of everything being racially separate, so it was unusual for a black woman and a white woman to click. Bonnie and I are clearly from two different worlds. But we didn't focus on what was different about us."

Their work with girls and women inspired them to write *Womantalk: A Guide to Life-Changing Communication*, which offers simple tips on how to have supportive conversations with friends. "Our book is not an empty set of words. It's something we live by," says Bonnie, who still calls on Ada today for friendship, support, and advice.

Ada Miller Robinson, left, and Bonnie Jackson Mitchell

Friendship Connections to Carry with You Always

You've heard of friendship bracelets, right? How about a friendship key chain or pendant—made from two connecting pieces of a jigsaw puzzle?

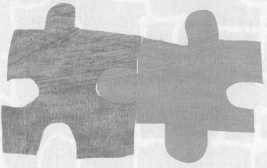

- From an old jigsaw puzzle, find two pieces you really like that fit together.

- On the back of each piece, write one word that describes an inner quality you value most in the friend you want to give this puzzle piece to.

- Coat both pieces (on each side) with clear fingernail polish or a clear acrylic spray.

- Let dry for 24 hours.

- Then punch a hole at the top of each piece.

- Slide one puzzle piece around your key ring, or hang it on a chain or cord for a necklace, and give the other to your friend as a reminder of your connection to her and what you value most about her.

Friendship
Mentorship

You and one or more friends could create a **Friendship Mentorship** group to educate and inspire younger girls about healthy friendships and sisterhood ideals.

If This Issue Speaks to You, Get Others Involved!

First, you and your friends might meet with a group of middle school girls from your neighborhood and ask to hang out with them. You might play games, go to a movie or the mall, or have a pizza party. No matter what you do, you and your friends would serve as role models of good friendship behavior for the younger girls. And each time you meet, you could talk about a friendship or a sisterhood issue that is of interest to the younger girls. So check with them! What matters most to them? What do they want some advice about?

Expand This into a Sisterhood Project!

Take your Friendship Mentorship wider!

- ☐ **Decide who your best audience might be and seek permission to work with them!** Do you want to work with a large group of younger girls at a local school, community center, or place of worship? Contact the proper officials (if a local middle school, the principal and perhaps teachers you know; if a community center, the director) to explain your plan and the great results you had when you tried it out informally.

- ☐ **Ask those officials for assistance in finding a larger group of girls who might want to improve sisterhood** and friendships in their middle school world. You might offer to meet once a week with girls for a set period of time (a month or two, or perhaps a season, such as during the winter months) to do fun things, and talk about what sisterhood means to them and can do for them. You could also discuss any sisterhood challenges the younger girls are facing.

- ☐ **Decide on some fun PR to get the girls excited about the first Friendship Mentorship meeting!** You might create a cool flier of fun friendship facts, put together an inviting PA announcement, or hold a creative friendship performance at lunchtime in the school cafeteria.

Keep Your Sisterhood Going!

Once you have a wider Friendship Mentorship going, consider expanding the reach of your project by helping the younger girls identify a sisterhood issue they want to resolve in their world (such as stopping catty talk among girls at school or learning how to find new, positive friends).

☐ **Then work with them** to create a plan to address the issue.

☐ **Once you settle on an issue**, you might even tackle it together through a Friendship Mixer (page 56) or a Circle Journal (page 64). Invite the girls you mentored to your Sisterhood Award celebration, and continue to mentor them on an as-needed basis. Remember, mentor relationships can evolve into real friendships, or future networking opportunities. See where yours take you!

Make the most of MISSION: SISTERHOOD!

As your Friendship Mentorship gets going, sprinkle in some fun stuff from *Mission: Sisterhood!*, such as the Friendship Connections accessories on page 42.

FRIENDSHIP WITHOUT BORDERS

chapter 4

YOU PROBABLY DON'T HAVE JUST ONE FRIEND

but belong to a larger group of friends. This means you have the opportunity to reach out to and take in from a variety of people. But how diverse is your group of friends, really? Do you share the same hobbies or interests, likes or dislikes? Do you even dress or look a little bit alike?

That wouldn't be unusual. People have a tendency to be drawn to people who are like them—in social status, values, ways of thinking, or even looks! In fact, it's much easier to form a relationship with someone who's like you.

So expanding your friendship borders might seem like wandering into uncharted territory. But opening yourself up to people who are different from you adds richness to your life. It will give you access to new ideas, interests, and challenges. It brings you new opportunities and alternative perspectives and can expand your network of sisters.

In Any Friendship, Tolerance Comes into Play!

Being tolerant doesn't mean compromising your beliefs, lifestyle, or safety. It means having a fair and objective attitude toward those who are different from you. A tolerant person understands that no two people have the same exact looks, beliefs, or ways of living, and that our differences make the world more interesting.

Practicing and understanding tolerance strengthens your relationships—and your ability to make new friends and be an effective leader. For example, one of your friends might come from another country, speak multiple languages, practice a faith different from your own, or listen to completely different music than you. Your being tolerant of these differences can be the first step to gaining some added richness in your life. You'll enjoy new interests and experiences, and you'll add a whole new layer to your sisterhood story. Plus, your inspiration will lead others!

Meditation Breakfast Shake

This shake is the perfect vehicle for tolerance! You can make it with fruit that is less than ripe or slightly overripe (but not spoiled!)—the kind you probably wouldn't tolerate eating raw! The more diverse the fruits you use, the more interesting and delicious your smoothie will be!

1. Wash, slice, and toss fruit in a blender. Try a mix of berries, tropical fruits, and stone fruits.
2. Add 1 scoop low-fat plain or vanilla yogurt and a handful of ice.
3. Add 2 ounces of juice or milk of your choice.
4. Blend until liquefied. Enjoy!

keep safety in sisterhood

When you're meeting new people in person or online, keep your standard safety checks in place:

- Keep meetings public.
- Be open but not too open! Don't divulge any personal information you wouldn't normally share with strangers.
- Take it slow: Real friendships develop over time.
- Trust your gut reactions: If something seems off, it probably is!

You might think of finding new friends as simply taking time to turn over a stone you see day after day but have never touched. Think of all the people you rub shoulders with every day—on the school bus, in the cafeteria, on the playing field.

The next time you pass by them, make the extra effort and strike up a conversation. How? Comment on ...

- the beautiful weather outside, or the latest news.
- something funny you both just saw happen.
- something you'd find interesting if someone said it to you!

When you consider all these new people each day, think about the diversity they might add to your sisterhood, and your life. You might consider diversity in many ways: age, gender, money matters ... turn the page to learn more!

Friendships Sewn Right In!

The 1995 movie "How to Make an American Quilt," based on the book by Whitney Otto, is about a young woman in graduate school (played by Winona Ryder), who joins her grandmother's quilting group and unexpectedly finds genuine friendship with these much older women.

Try this: List more friendship movies where unexpected friendships blossom, if you can think of any, and get together with your friends to host a friendship screening.

Age

How many people do you know who never saw a computer until they were in midlife? People older than you can help you understand life and values from a historical perspective. They can also offer advice and assistance. People younger than you can help you understand life from their perspective. And you can offer *them* advice!

Where to meet people of various ages? Everywhere! The park, the grocery store, the pet shop, a charity run, your place of worship. Find them and strike up a conversation using the icebreaker tips on page 56.

Gender

Gender can get in the way when guys and girls want to be friends but fear that their friendship might be rumored to be romantic. To avoid this, always send clear signals to your guy friend. Is your body language and talk flirty or romantically suggestive? If you keep it fun but business-like, you won't tangle over any mixed signals. And remember to respect your gender differences!

Money Matters

Money-related differences can create a real barrier in friendships, so be sensitive when making friends with someone from an economic background different from your own. Be careful about how you plan to get together—will you pack a lunch or eat out? Take in a movie or enjoy some quiet time in a park? Don't make assumptions (like, money buys happiness) and don't stereotype. No matter what side of the coin you're on, there's a story behind each girl, and you could have more in common, or more to learn, than meets the eye.

Special Interests

Your current friends probably like to do a lot of things that you like to do. Perhaps you met while working on the school newspaper. But you may have additional interests that you never thought of sharing with them. For example, you might enjoy hiking but know they'd rather traverse the mountains of clothing at the mall. So you never bothered to suggest going on a hike. But don't ignore what interests you, explore it! This gives you a chance to expand your friends' worlds. And who knows? You might all find even more new friends in the process.

Expand Your Sisterhood—and Exercise, Too!

Why not help a good cause, get exercise, and hang out with some new sisters all at one time? Sign up for a charity walk, run, or bike ride today!

Looks

Do you ever feel like someone doesn't want to be your friend because of the way you look or dress? How does it feel? Not great, because you know that you are so much more than just what your physical appearance might say on a particular day. So, if you ever find yourself avoiding someone based on their looks, redirect your thoughts! Look at the whole person. Do you like this person's manner (toward you and toward others), her interests, her abilities? All of these things are far more important considerations than looks when trying to expand your friendship borders!

Labels

It's easy to stereotype and label a group, such as jocks, cheerleaders, or band geeks, but if you narrow down a group of people to one quality and a derogatory way of expressing it, you're not seeing the true colors of each individual. So instead of saying, "She's a jock," try, "She likes sports and likes to hang out with others who have that interest." Instead of a label, you're describing what that person enjoys or does often. What else does she like? Take time to find out and you'll be less likely to label her—you might even find a new friend!

A Promise You Can Shape

You may have heard it a zillion times or maybe this is the first time: "On my honor, I will try to serve God . . . "

Girl Scouts doesn't define or interpret the word "God" in the Girl Scout Promise. Instead, individual members establish for themselves the nature of their spiritual beliefs. That's the Girl Scout way!

Striving to live by the Promise and Law is one thing you have in common with all your Girl Scout sisters. This is true no matter what your spiritual beliefs.

Make Friends Near and Far

Continue the spirit of global friendship and leadership by connecting with other Girl Scouts and Girl Guides through the World Association of Girl Guides and Girl Scouts (WAGGGS). You may even find ideas to support your Sisterhood Project.

Religion

Luckily, many girls find it easy to befriend people whose spiritual beliefs differ from their own. But if your beliefs are vastly different, and you find yourself putting up barriers to your friendship, you might do some research. You might be surprised at the many ways that various religions actually see eye to eye! (Think of the Golden Rule, for one! If you haven't yet enjoyed the *GIRLtopia* leadership journey, check it out, especially page 45.) The more you know about what connects you, and what sets you apart, the more confident and comfortable you, and your friends, will feel.

Language

Hearing and speech differences, from disabilities to accents and speaking an entirely different language, can create challenges when forming a friendship. They can also lead to miscommunications and confusion.

If a foreign language is the barrier, draw pictures, speak slowly, rephrase, ask more questions, use body language and expression, and admit when you don't understand instead of pretending that you do. You can become closer by teaching each other words in your respective languages.

Getting by with a Little Help from Friends

When **Dallas Jessup** was 13, she learned the unsettling statistics that 1 in 4 girls are sexually assaulted and 114,000 attempted abductions occur each year in the United States. So Dallas, who had earned a black belt in tae kwon do, set out to make a movie to teach her classmates some defensive street fighting moves. Thanks to her networking savvy and marketing skills, her idea went well beyond its initial brainstorm. Sixty days after word got out, she had more than 100 volunteers, celebrity cameos lined up, and $600,000 in donated resources. She raised money to film "Just Yell Fire," then posted the video online, and sent DVDs to girls worldwide who lacked Internet access. Dallas' work has since reached girls in 45 countries—that's a big sisterhood!

Dallas has since lobbied for mandatory teen-safety school programs, and she speaks at campuses, law enforcement conferences, and crisis shelters. On her travels, especially at scholarship and award events, Dallas forges new friendships that add to the richness of her life. "We're all making a difference and using our strengths," she says. "It's important to network and collaborate with each other. I met a guy who was bringing supplies to a rural village in India. He helped me organize my own trip to India, where I spoke to college women about sex-trafficking awareness."

Dallas, now 17, credits many mentors with helping make her video successful, especially her mom. "She mostly asked questions, and that's what you want in a mentor. You don't want someone to do the thinking for you," Dallas says.

Women in Film

This organization supports, promotes, and mentors women in the entertainment industries by funding scholarships and internships, assisting independent filmmakers, and hosting events and seminars to educate and enlighten.

Friendship Mixer

By now you understand the value of broadening friendship borders—for yourself and for others. If you want to spread the positive message of broadening friendship borders, organizing a **Friendship Mixer** might be a great idea. A Friendship Mixer is like a friendship match-making party; it's an event where a diverse group of girls can meet, share stories, and make meaningful friendship connections. The idea is to encourage girls to be open to diversity in all of their relationships, and to give them the opportunity to get to know others they wouldn't normally meet or seek out—not just on this one day but throughout their lives.

Friendship Mixer Icebreaker Questions

Try some of these and add in your own!

- If you won the lottery, what would you do?
- If you had a magic wand, what would you change?
- What are your five favorite possessions in life?
- If you could be anyone in the world, past or present, who would you be?

If This Issue Speaks to You, Get Others Involved and Make It Your Sisterhood Project!

Host a Friendship Mixer. You can do this alone, with a buddy or with your group of Seniors.

Decide how you want to run the Mixer. Ask the girls to complete short questionnaires describing their interests, hobbies, and passions? Write fun ice breaker questions for them to ask one another? Randomly assign girls teams to complete a scavenger hunt?

- ☐ Arrange the time and place, send invitations, and advertise it to as many girls as possible.

- ☐ Before the Mixer, prepare any needed items, like icebreaker questions.

- ☐ Have index cards, or fun, mini-"address books" and pens available for girls to share contact information with one another, and encourage them to do so.

Keep Your Sisterhood Going!

Figure out a way to take your Friendship Mixer on the road—to schools, community centers, your Girl Scout council—so it reaches even more girls!

CIRCLE THE WORLD FOR SISTERHOOD

chapter 5

YOU PROBABLY HAVE ALREADY STARTED

expanding your network and spreading the benefits of sisterhood beyond your community borders. So how can you take this collective power even further? How can you make use of this network to take action on behalf of all your sisters, near and far?

Juliette Gordon Low brought Girl Scouts to the United States because she believed that action for sisterhood would blossom if girls around the world connected as sisters who wanted to make the world better. As you expand your sisterhood circle globally, through either relationships or shared concerns, think about how much more you and your new sisters can accomplish, and how much more powerful you are together. There's strength in numbers—and in a sisterhood of leaders acting together!

Consider your Sisterhood Project. When you first started thinking about it, did you take into account a variety of diverse perspectives? Or did you rely on perspectives from your immediate circle?

Can you now go further in how you educate and inspire others about your project and the issue it seeks to address? After all, the issue may be important to people well beyond even your expanded circle—it may be an issue important throughout the world! Can you harness your sisterhood power and expand your network's reach even further?

Sisterhood
Time Capsule

With a friend or with your group, gather together some news stories (online or newspapers) about sisterhood issues you care about. You might find stories about:

- a girl who experienced dating violence.
- the daughter of a financially strapped single parent who has to take on all the household chores.
- young girls denied education in developing countries.
- girls facing discrimination in classrooms or on sports fields.

Something to Try with Your Circle

Imagine putting these stories in a time capsule that will be unearthed by a future generation of Girl Scout Seniors. How do you envision these sisterhood stories influencing and inspiring girls over future decades? Is the story of sisterhood better? In what way?

Maybe you and your friends want to organize a multiregional Time Capsule event to better understand how perspectives vary on the most important sisterhood issues of the day. You'll learn what other girls put in their time capsules and how your concerns are similar to or different from those of girls in other regions. If you find recurring issues or themes, perhaps you can band together to get some change going on a larger scale.

Doing a Sisterhood Time Capsule is also a great way to find a sisterhood issue toward your award!

Her Cause Is
Your Cause!

Shannon, center, with her mentor, Smart Baitani, left, and Justina Rwebogora, headmistress at Kiteyagwa Primary School in Tanzania.

Shannon McNamara, a 15-year-old from Basking Ridge, New Jersey, gave power to sisterhood by putting together two facts she learned about girls in Tanzania, Africa: Many girls there drop out after grade school to earn money for their families. But one year of secondary school can raise the wages these girls are able to earn by as much as 25 percent. Shannon's After-School Reading Exchange (SHARE), which keeps girls learning, has since changed the lives of girls in three Tanzanian locations!

Shannon's project, which earned her a Girl Scout Gold Award, is great inspiration for a Sisterhood Project. Shannon received invaluable assistance from a mentor—Smart Baitani, cofounder and executive director of Compassionate Solutions for Africa's Development. "We started to exchange e-mails," Shannon says. "Our similar goal to help the girls connected us together."

Volunteers were also key: Classmates collected books and labeled and boxed them for shipment. Girl Scout groups and libraries pitched in, too. Best of all, Shannon really changed lives across borders.

"In July 2008, on my first trip to Tanzania, some girls wouldn't look me in the eye and were nervous," Shannon recalls. "When I came back one year later, they started screaming and hugging me. Their confidence had improved and they talked to me in English and Swahili."

sisterhood in Action

"My fight began with a promise I made to my sister Suzy to do everything I could to find a cure for breast cancer. When Suzy was first diagnosed, the world was much different. . . . There was no Internet. There were no information hotlines. There were no global campaigns to educate people and spread awareness."

—Nancy G. Brinker, on keeping her promise and her connection to her sister, who died in 1980, by founding the Susan G. Komen for the Cure foundation, the largest source of nonprofit funds dedicated to fighting breast cancer.

Random Act of Sisterhood!

Leave a favorite friendship book in a place that teen girls frequent (a locker room at school, for example) with a note that says, "If you are a teen girl: Read me, then pass me on." In the front of the book, include a link to a Web page you might have created, where girls who read the book are invited to log on, review the book, and tell a story about friendship. (They can also share where they found the book and where they might leave it for the next person.)

Three books to consider:

Pride and Prejudice by Jane Austen

The Running Dream by Wendelin Van Draanen

The Secret Life of Bees by Sue Monk Kidd

Try This for Fun!
Circle Journal

A circle journal is another great way to keep your sisterhood growing— and one of the easiest ways to grow it around the world. It's basically a journal that two or more people pass back and forth, with each person contributing her own entries. A circle journal is a fun and creative way to get to know other people and issues of importance to them.

Consider identifying a global sisterhood issue and creating a circle journal to support it. Think of the collective power you can harness if you share a concern globally! You'll learn what issues girls in other regions care about. If you find recurring issues, perhaps you can band together to get some change going on a larger scale.

By reaching out to other girls in this way, you are being a sister to girls you don't even know.

Sisterhood:
Keep Your Circle Growing

Sisterhood has the power to change you and change the world. You've seen how growing your sisterhood circle not only gives you more friends, it gives you more opportunities to be a leader in your own life and in the world. It makes your world wider and more diverse, and it fills it with an awareness and understanding of sisterhood needs and the many ways you can band with your sisters to fill those needs.

You can now count yourself among the many girls and women who have made a difference for sisterhood. You've read about some in this book, like Shannon McNamara, Dallas Jessup, Bonnie Jackson Mitchell, and Ada Miller Robinson.

Many other women have moved sisterhood to where it is today, thanks to their service to their country, their advocacy for equal rights for women, and their ability to push the boundaries in terms of what women can do. To name just a few examples:
- abolitionists Sojourner Truth and Harriet Tubman
- suffragettes Elizabeth Cady Stanton and Susan B. Anthony
- U.S. Secretaries of State Condoleezza Rice and Hillary Clinton
- Supreme Court Justices Sandra Day O'Connor and Sonia Sotomayor
- women's rights activists Gloria Steinem and Betty Friedan
- the first female U.S. ambassador to the United Nations Jeane Kirkpatrick

They all started the story of sisterhood, and now it's up to you to keep it going and growing.

What sisters in the present and in history have inspired you along your journey? Celebrate their stories—and yours! In what ways will you continue to pave the way for sisters worldwide?

Take some time to savor all you accomplished on this journey.

In what ways will you stay connected to the sisters who joined your network along this journey?

Where will you take your sisterhood and where will it take you?

As you move ahead, you'll find many ways to strengthen all of the values you've **Discovered** along this journey. You'll also find ways to act on those values and infuse them into how you **Take Action** to champion sisterhood issues now and throughout your life.

Connecting with others to promote sisterhood and all the causes tied to it is how you'll strengthen your power. You'll have expanded your reach and increased your opportunities to Take Action, and those two things together amplify your impact. In this way, your sisterhood continues to educate and inspire an ever-widening circle all around you.

MISSION: SISTERHOOD! is a journey that offers you a lifetime of opportunities to be a leader who makes a difference. **So share the story of your journey and how it changed the lives of others—and you!**

My Sisterhood
Project Planner

A Lifelong Tool for
Getting Through Any Project!

To reach Mission: Accomplished! you will:

1. Define a sisterhood issue for yourself.

You've seen a lot of sisterhood issues you can Take Action on. You've read about women and girls who have acted on sisterhood issues important to them. Maybe you tried the Sisterhood Time Capsule or Circle Journal and new issues presented themselves to you. Maybe you've started to take notice of issues around you, in your own life, and in your community, too.

The sample Sisterhood Projects throughout the journey suggest possible sisterhood issues to tackle. They also step you through how to plan a Sisterhood Project that will have positive impact:

- Finding the Beauty in Images of Beauty, page 20
- Call Out That Inner Beauty, page 32
- Friendship Mentorship, page 43
- Friendship Mixer, page 56

But the sample projects are just that—samples. Use your creativity to find your own! Ask around: What issues are women and girls passionate about in your community?

So it's time to grab your sisterhood issue! What might it be?

As you weigh your options, keep in mind that **a great Sisterhood Project gives you the opportunity to:**

- find and think about a sisterhood issue you've never thought about before
- figure out what you can do about a sisterhood issue you care about
- meet and talk to new people (which expands your sisterhood!)
- understand how to focus your efforts so you get results despite whatever time and resource obstacles you might face
- start some change that keeps on going even after you're done
- step back and say, "I made this change happen!"
- be a true example of sisterhood in action!

I've identified my issue!

It's _____

_____

_____

_____

How Will You Find a Sisterhood Cause to Take

The best place to start looking for your sisterhood issue is right in a sisterhood. Start with your Girl Scout friends—what projects are they planning? Check out your council website—what are girls in your area doing? Go to ForGirls.GirlScouts.org and click on "Map It!," where you can see how other girls around the country are changing the world with their projects. And go online to research how Girl Scouts and Girl Guides are taking action on a global scale.

2. Develop Your Mission!

Decide on the results you want to see.

The specific results I will aim for are:

_____

_____

_____

_____

_____

Remember, your Sisterhood Project can be big or small.

But whatever the size, keep it focused! A focused project has the most potential for great impact. Choose the size and scope that fits your passion and your time. A project of any size can make a great impact if it is well-planned and well-focused!

To get these results, I will need to talk to and involve these people:

_____

_____

_____

_____

_____

I will also need to do some research about these things:

_____

_____

_____

_____

Now that you know your issue and what you hope to accomplish, create a commercial for your issue. If you have only 30 seconds to explain your issue, why it matters, and what you're going to do about it, what would you say?

That's **Your Mission**.

Jot it here:

_____

_____

_____

_____

_____

_____

Don't Forget Your Younger Sisters!

Consider a Sisterhood Project that directly involves younger Girl Scouts. You've got one idea on page 43, the Friendship Mentorship. But you can think up plenty more on your own. You might even team up with Girl Scout Juniors enjoying the *aMUSE It's Your Story—Tell It!* Journey, which has them educating and inspiring others about how to stop stereotypes from limiting the roles girls and women can take on in life.

3. Make the Big Decisions!

Now that you have a mission, you need to get specific about how and for whom you will carry it out. **Who will you educate and inspire? Or who will you advocate for? What will you educate and inspire others about?** These decisions are the beginning of your Sisterhood Project plan!

It may be that by focusing in on one aspect of your issue, you'll get greater results than if you go big and broad with your efforts. Think of a snowball—what change do you want to put in motion, and how can you involve others so that this change grows and grows? Use the questions and the space in this planner to start creating your own sisterhood spiral!

4. Logistics Time!

Consider each of the following:

The scope of your project: How many people are you reaching out to? Are they local, nationwide, or abroad?

Example: I might start my project at my sister's school but see if later I can expand it to other middle schools in our district.

YOUR IDEAS HERE:

_____

_____

_____

_____

_____

Your resources: What people, supplies, money, and in-kind donations will you need? Do you have a budget? Will there be any costs to cover? Even fliers cost money! How can you keep costs down or eliminate them entirely? Who can you ask for donations?

Example: I'll have 300 fliers to print; if I take this online, I'll have URL registration and hosting fees. Maybe a local business will cover my costs? Maybe an existing Web site will loan me space free of charge?

YOUR IDEAS HERE:

_____

_____

_____

_____

Tips for sisterhood!

As you work through your logistics, if you find yourself getting stressed that you don't have enough time or resources, that's a sign that perhaps you need to go back to your early "what-can-I-do" thinking and focus your efforts even tighter or shift things around a little.

For example, is there something you can do that fits into your school day?

PR/marketing: You might ask a public relations expert for tips on …

- creating fliers that explain why your issue is important.
- writing a pitch letter to a radio or TV news station about your project.

YOUR IDEAS HERE:

Engage as many people as possible, as either mentors or volunteers. Depending on the topic of your project, you might:

- Talk to a psychologist, social worker, or counselor about how to write girl-to-girl mentorship questions, and ask for their assistance checking facts for any informational fliers you might create.

- Ask girls with healthy friendship and sisterhood values/skills to volunteer as mentors.

- Ask a graphic designer for advice on attention-grabbing fliers.

- Ask teachers if you can receive school credit for any aspects of your project. Perhaps a math teacher can assist with statistics or an English teacher can help you write the fliers?

- Talk to students interested in filmmaking to see if they would create a mini documentary on your project, which you can then use to promote your project and expand its reach.

YOUR IDEAS HERE:

Support Your Cause Creatively!

One of the most powerful ways to educate and inspire others is through creative expression. You can tell the story of your cause, or the story that illustrates the need for it, through any art form—dance, drama, music, the written word, or visual art of any kind. For example, Dallas Jessup (see page 54) made a video to show girls how to defend themselves against attackers. What creative medium would you choose? A play? A dance? A music performance? A blog? Aim for something that will stretch your creativity and showcase your individual talents!

Your efforts will be strengthened by numbers!
The more dedicated sisters you have, the more momentum your project will have. That means your project's possibilities for success will be greater, too! (And don't forget the brothers. If you don't have the guys involved, you won't have made much change in a world of two sexes!)

Don't Forget to . . .

Embrace Your Mistakes!
Learn from them! Focus on what you do that works. There's so much you want to change and accomplish, so it's important to appreciate every small accomplishment along the way.

5. Creating the Project Timeline

IMPORTANT DATES	WHAT MUST HAPPEN	WHO'S RESPONSIBLE	notes

What will Happen Next?

Ask yourself, "So what will happen when I am done?" Build something into your plan that helps the spiral grow. For example, if your project is with younger girls, you might ask them to do something else to pass it on. Or perhaps a teacher in your school could help make whatever you started a monthly happening.

What will you set in motion so that your spiral can keep on going even when you are done? After all, sisterhood doesn't end when your award project ends!

Real Results for Sisterhood!

Check back here when your work is done! What results did you see?

Real Reflection for Sisterhood!

What did you learn that you are most excited about?

Who did you meet? (Anyone you need to thank? Any loose ends dangling?)

What might you change or do differently next time?

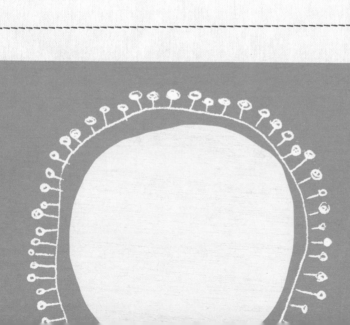

Real Rewards for Sisterhood!

Time to add your pin to your collection of achievements!
This is a symbol of all you have achieved through and for sisterhood.
But what does earning the Sisterhood Award really mean to you?

Here's what it means in Girl Scouts:

You are a sister who has DISCOVERED her values and how to act
on them. You've also CONNECTED with a circle of sisters and
TAKEN ACTION to help change the world—you are a leader!

Sisterhood—keep the spiral growing!